GNOSIS OF THE HEART

Gnosis of the Heart

Carroll Blair

Aveon Publishing Company

ISBN: 978-1-936430-25-3

Library of Congress Control Number
2011907213

Aveon Publishing Co.
P.O. Box 380739
Cambridge, MA 02238-0739 USA

Also by Carroll Blair

Grains of Thought
Facing the Circle
Reel to Real
Shifting Tides
Reaches
Out of Silence
Quarter Notes
By Rays of Light
Into the Inner Life
Soul Reflections
Beneath and Beyond the Surface
Of Courage and Commitment
For Today and Tomorrow
In Meditation
Sightings Along the Journey
Through Desert's Fire
Offerings to Pilgrims
Human Natures
(Of Animal and Spiritual)
Atoms from the Suns of Solitude
Colors of Devotion
Voicings
Through the Shadows
As the World Winds Flow

Humanity was born the moment the first human acted with consideration for another not of the same tribe or blood.

It has been said that the genius of one age could not flourish in every age because of differences of circumstance and environment, the hypothesis seeming to be correct, but the great virtues of the heart, one might say its genius, are the same in all ages, their qualities being eternal, expressing themselves throughout time, as essential to human existence in one time as in another, their power always ready to serve, ever to fill the lives of those who choose to embrace them.

The humble heart, the compassionate heart, the noble heart are all one, doing the work of love.

Life as a human being does not begin until empathy is fully present in one's being.

As the ego diminishes the heart begins to blossom, the cover of selfishness breaking down opening one's life to growth, to love, to light.

One's life expands to the measure of its giving.

The motives that drive compassion are void of self-interest, yet serve the interest of all.

Peace is not enough, wisdom must also be present; wisdom is not enough, love must also be present.

Love is the sole entity that has the power
to turn evil toward the light of goodness
and error toward the light of truth.

As love takes from one it gives to one,
filling one with the desire to keep giving.

The hand doesn't realize it's full sensation
until touched by another hand; the heart, until
touched by another heart.

Your life is not about you, *cannot be* about "you" if you are to achieve wholeness as a human being.

The noble heart is free of the desire to rule over others, to control others, to exploit or manipulate others . . . it is only interested in serving, in loving, in giving to others all that it has to give.

To be evolving spiritually is to be open to the offering of oneself every moment of one's life.

If your ego is not diminishing, your love
not increasing, you are not growing; and
if you are not growing, how can you be
living in the higher sense — (in the
spiritual sense . . .)

When one lives for something more than
oneself life seems so much stronger in its
magnificence.

The heart of humanity does not feed the
individual heart — it is the individual heart
that must bring love and light to the heart
of humanity one by one, nourishing it,
keeping it alive.

Great can be the gift of even the smallest act of kindness.

Every day throughout humankind countless opportunities to perform a simple act of kindness are passed by that can sometimes mean the world to someone, and even change their world.

What is more moving or mesmerizing than the beauty of love . . .

Love takes on all shapes and forms.
No place is too small or too large for its
presence — it goes everywhere it is invited,
and sometimes not invited. Its giving is
infinite, the commitment of its devotion,
tireless, generated by the divine force
of which it is made.

Love and Selflessness go more than hand and
hand — they are inseparably joined as one.

The path to Selflessness . . . shedding the ego
bit by bit, every step of the way.

There is always more one can do for others; there is always more one can do for life.

The selfless motive is the jewel of human character.

Motive is as cloud or sunshine to the manifests of action.

Righteousness comes from purity of heart.

Even more than the mind the enlightened heart knows what is right.

There is always advantage in some way gained when one refrains from taking advantage of another.

One uses one's life badly when using other people.

Whatever one does to another for ill or good one does to the world, for all are part of the world.

If one is not good to others what right has one to be good to himself?

What one says is as important as what one does regarding gestures of kindness and cruelty.

Where there is malice nothing good or noble can ever exist.

Malice: the most corrosive toxin of human entity.

It is fear more than ignorance that closes a mind and prevents a heart from growing.

Courage is the virtue that raises all other virtues, the attribute that expands all other attributes.

Ego is a prison that many fear to dismantle, because it is also a place to hide.

The more self-centered people are the less centered they are, spiritually speaking.

One cannot begin to have *human* contact with another human being until one is free from the silent question "What can this person do for me?"

Until there is nothing you want from another you cannot *see* him, cannot *see* her.

Objectively speaking self-worth begins where
self-interest ends.

It is no gift that one gives to another who gives
with the hope or expectation of receiving
something in return.

The enlightened heart does everything,
gives everything in the spirit of love.

What is not selfless in emanation is without depth or noble substance.

The most barren of lives are those that are thoroughly consumed with the care and preservation of themselves.

To acquire wealth, any kind of wealth, including spiritual, only for oneself is to create a poverty of one's self.

True gain is always aligned with giving.

The light of one's life is only as bright
as the beauty in one's heart.

The heart that truly loves is always
filled with love.

What can a mind or spirit become or ever be raised to without the assistance of a loving heart?

One earns one's life by serving others, by serving life.

The great gift given to an individual is diminished when not utilized for the benefit of others.

Who does little beyond his own bidding
is not only missing life, but also his life.

To learn what it means to love . . . the
primary lesson of humanity.

One cannot live beyond the animal of
human-being until one can truly love.

To not be compassionate toward all living things as far as possible is to not be living through the spiritual of human-being (which is to not be experiencing the best of human life).

Compassion is not only for those who are of the highest quality of character, which is one of the reasons it is among the highest qualities of human character.

One cannot always count upon the better nature of others, if it is present, or has even been developed; one can only cultivate one's own and do one's best to make its presence felt in everything that one does.

The more enlightened one is, the more grateful he or she is to realize where they've been wrong than where they've been right.

It is much easier to forgive a mistake than a refusal to admit to one made.

What you are unable to own up to, owns you.

Overlooking an error by another when one doesn't have to may be virtuous (e.g., when there is no personal loss or gain at stake), but at no time under any circumstance is it virtuous to overlook an error of one's own.

People cannot viably think themselves to be honest until they are ashamed of being dishonest with themselves.

There is no greater aid to peace of mind than knowing you have done your best to do what is best.

When there are other people involved,
getting what you want is never honorable
if not also fair to the other person(s).

Fairness in human affairs is more a matter
of compassion than it is justice. It depends
on the integrity, fair-mindedness and generosity of the ones who hold a position of
authority, and how they choose to wield
their power or advantage.

It is more important to be worthy of whatever
fortune may come into your life than it is to
have it.

An evil in the world that is practiced daily
is the wants of some, taking from the needs
of others.

How superior the generous heart is to the
scheming, manipulative mind.

To hoard the world's bread [material wealth]
is to be starved of spiritual wealth.

The ubiquity and tolerance of man's smaller evils are what enable his larger evils to manifest.

Unlike evil, nothing good can be done by weakness.

.

How much fear lives in the hearts of those who are always looking out for themselves.

True freedom is acquired by committing oneself to the service of love, of truth, of life.

They need the least from life who give all that they have to give.

Love is impossible to keep to oneself. One who is filled with it must constantly give it away.

They haven't the mind for great wisdom
who haven't the heart for great love.

Like the highest wisdom, the highest love
is beyond its expression.

Few profoundly realize how great the privilege
to love.

Love too is something that must be
aspired to.

To improve one's life is to make oneself
better, hence making the lives of those
around one better.

The stronger a life becomes the more caring
and generous it becomes.

The open heart expands, growing further into light.

They cannot lose who live a life of kindness and generosity; they cannot win despite illusions to the contrary who live a life of greed and selfishness.

To always do right by others is to not only honor their lives, but to also honor life.

It is not possible for anyone to strip another of his or her dignity, but one sheds part of one's own in the process of trying.

To achieve true power (i.e., spiritual power) is to achieve the state of being where one is free from all desire to have power over others.

The more ego one possesses the more in the dark one is.

One's life is necessary only so far as it is necessary to the service of life outside itself.

Where there is humility there is growth, and room for higher growth.

Love brings all possibilities within reach.

When a way cannot be found love cannot
be present.

The way is clear to the open heart.

Love is all-giving, yet also demanding of
the hearts that are its agents, doing a work
that is never ending.

Everywhere one goes in the world love and kindness are needed — never can there be too much, and almost everywhere there is not enough.

A sadness surfaces and one turns away from it instead of going to it, adding another sadness to the world.

Man is imprisoned by his evil and freed by his goodness.

Without goodness of heart it is not possible to be *alive* in the profoundest sense of human life.

Just as man is able to raise himself above the animal world by certain attributes of his being, so can he fall beneath it by giving himself over to the baser elements of his being.

Like other animals, humans can sense weakness or vulnerability in others, but to act on this instinct when there is no threat or danger to oneself, or take advantage of it for personal gain or sport at the expense of others who have not agreed to participate in whatever game is being played is to operate from the lower levels rather than the higher (the spiritual) of human-being.

Integrity of mind and integrity of spirit are
inexorably linked, their essence determined
by the nature of the heart.

To be enlightened is to do one's best to always
be helpful, never harmful to others.

It never profits a man's heart or soul when his
mind turns to obsession for profit.

To not give others their proper due or acknowledgement according to their merit(s) is to take something from them.

When one wrongfully takes something away from another one also takes something more costly away from oneself.

They never know how much they harm themselves who willfully harm others.

Among the most toxic and evil are those who feel good when making others feel bad.

They give the most pain to others who haven't the courage to face their pain.

When evil is committed the heart of humankind suffers, the wound healed only by gestures of love.

It is not uncommon for the most wronged
to be among the most forgiving.

Sometimes the tears shed by a victim of an
offense are not for the victim, but for the
offender, for what the offender has done to
himself by the evil of his transgression.
This unusual sentiment (especially if the
offender is a stranger to the victim) is the
rarest and highest form of compassion —
a display or example of Christ-like or
Buddha-like compassion.

Remorse for an offense against another
is only the beginning of expiation.

A genuine apology is always followed by genuine action or change for the better.

One adds a positive to the world who removes a negative from within.

It is often the means life forces correction on ignoble behavior is also essential to the work of salvation.

True redemption is never about concern for oneself, but making amends to the party or parties that one has injured.

To apologize for the wrong reason is to add an offense to the one for which an apology has been given.

Intent is as important to the moral measure as deed or gesture. To do right or seek to amend out of fear of retribution or loss to oneself if one does not is far from the spirit of atonement.

You do a greater wrong to the one who has injured you than the injury committed against you if you are able to teach the offender to do better, and do not.

How great the difference of maturity of heart between the following two states of thought: "I think with regret about those whom I have harmed, not of the offenses of those who have harmed me." "I think with anger about those who have harmed me, not with sorrow about those whom I have harmed."

The chances for growth are small so long as the ego is large.

It is more important to always do right than to always be right.

To look upon all human beings as persons with their own thoughts, feelings and aspirations instead of objects to be used solely for one's interests is to become (by that one change of perception) a better human being.

One needn't be a thinker per se to be thoughtful of others.

It is the character of the heart that sounds the alarm (or fails to) when one begins to compromise others or oneself.

All goodness turns in the direction of magnanimity.

The mindset of some is that life is for the taking; of others, for the giving.

The weight of greed gravely lowers the one who is consumed by it; the love of selflessness raises the spirit of one who has embraced it.

Good things await or follow the sincere effort for the advancement of the good.

It is they who do not know love who assume that in order to survive they must dominate.

Lost is the one who doesn't care if he is wrong or right providing that others believe him to be right.

Some walk through life as a ray of light; others as a shade of darkness.

The spirit that houses an able mind but an empty heart is not a spirit blessed.

One discovers life when coming to the realization that one's life is not about oneself, and generates value objectively only to the degree it is used as a vehicle for giving.

Whatever one has to give to life one owes it to life to give, yet once done it is the giver who feels honored, blessed to have been granted the opportunity to contribute, realizing that here lies the principal gift of human life.

One needs to do better than just doing better for oneself.

A million miles away from compassion
or an inch away . . . what is the difference?

Battles that are fought solely for personal
gain and not something higher are never
worth the fight, for one always loses, even
if the battle is won.

One doesn't move forward but backward
no matter what direction one is moving
when not helping others along the journey.

"All right," many say of this, of that, without doing what is right.

It is a gift of no small measure to recognize the error of one's ways.

Just as an ailing heart of the body affects the whole health of the body, so an ailing heart of the spirit affects the whole health of the spirit.

The healthy (enlightened) heart is the one whose time is spent tending to the needs of the world in little ways every day, and sometimes larger ways when the opportunity arises.

You want to feel better — are you doing better, and for the better . . . you want to feel good — are you doing good, and for the good . . .

A worthier goal than to "set the world on fire" is to add to it some warmth and light.

It is not how many lives you reach with what you do that matters but how many lives you touch.

At the end of one's life what does anything count for but what one has contributed to life?

Everyone is able to give something to others, and the kind word of one given to another can be worth more or do more good than many dollars of another given to someone else.

All this competition in youth, sharpening one's claws . . . yes — but what will they be used for? To tear at the evil, or the good of the world . . .

The enlightened heart makes love both the cause and the effect of its constitution.

There is no such thing as death with dignity where there has not been life with integrity.

The life well lived does not lament the coming of its winter, welcoming it as the blossom of youth welcoming the spring.

If one is always genuine one will not always be right, but one will never go wrong regarding the direction of one's life.

No matter what, there is always much to be thankful for; no matter what, there is always more to be done.

Fret not the love that goes unanswered, for it has fulfilled its purpose of being given.

A little love has the power to send much sorrow away.

The noblest aim of the heart is not to be loved, or to fall in love, but to *be* love, imparting benevolence and light to all that it may.

When one looks to the best of humankind one discovers the heart at its center.

The profoundest lessons of how to live the most human life are also the simplest, and come from the heart.

The greatest benefits manifest when acting without selfish motive.

The selfless motive must always be pure . . .
a single drop of oil can spoil many gallons
of clean water.

Perhaps the things that require the most ego
to achieve are the things least worthy of pursuit,
objectively speaking.

When the base and the banal are pursued
the more prevalent becomes the darkness within
the closer one is to the goal.

If one turns away from light there is still light. One needs to only open one's eyes . . . open one's heart.

Ego detests light. It does its work in the dark, and convinces many a lost soul that he is standing in the light.

In the end it all must be about love, or it is about nothing.

Until the question in one's mind regarding life changes from "What can I get?" to "How can I help, what can I give?" one hasn't begun to learn what love is.

To not learn certain things in life's journey and be humbled by them is to remain in the lower stratums of human-being.

It is not about making oneself "feel good about oneself," but making oneself better — which in turn creates depths in one's life where a sense of wellness beyond the fleeting can take root.

The primary task of every person who takes a serious interest in self-improvement is to try to be a better human being today than one was yesterday.

Every day, moving on, moving through, moving to the way of transcendence.

Do not all have a duty to do their best to raise humankind to its best?

It might be said that one doesn't have the right to jeopardize the best that is in one, or the promise of its realization.

The major challenge of human existence and triumph when succeeding is the overcoming of the predominance of animal nature in the ruling of one's existence.

An underdeveloped human being in the spiritual sense is a more tragic phenomenon than it is in the physical.

The feeling that one cannot live for self-gratification alone . . . the beginning of what makes possible the seeding of virtue in the heart of a human being.

Some believe that life is a gift given to them to (above all) enjoy themselves; others believe it is a gift that they in turn must give to something more than the pursuit of their own self-interests, to be given to something greater than themselves.

The more evolved one becomes, the more people and things one includes in one's reflections on considering how an action or series of actions one is contemplating will impact them, genuinely concerned for the wellness of life extending beyond oneself.

"If I cause you pain I hope it is the kind that brings you spiritual gold, i.e., insight and truth." (This, the sentiment of the enlightened heart.)

To pull one's punches without an opponent's knowledge that one is doing so is no small gesture of magnanimity.

When one is no longer pleased to be right in proving another wrong, one has cause to be pleased for the personal growth this represents.

The good that is done quietly, without seeking fanfare or applause speaks loudly for the state of heart from where it has come.

What comes from a high place of integrity chooses the low profile when able.

The feigning of virtue debases more than the genuine vice.

True kindness and generosity is never a showing of oneself to be kind and generous.

There are those who say many things by heart, but none of their expressions come from the heart.

Some cannot speak with love because they've never heard the voice of Love, though many times they have heard the words "I love you."

To deny what is true is never a part of love.

Hope is more than a fantasy only in the absence of greed, arrogance, deceit, selfishness; only in the presence of love, humility, selflessness.

To keep what one doesn't need is to be needy in attributes of spirit and heart.

Only when giving more than one has to, doing more than one has to is one doing close to enough.

The more ego is diminished the greater the capacity to love grows within.

The wise starve the ego, for they know that when allowed to feed it feeds on the best of them.

One cannot extend a free hand to others if inside oneself one is not free.

Your life is nothing without you, but it is also nothing if it is only about you.

What is the good of having wisdom, of having love, and all blessings of life if they are not shared or passed on to others?

Compassion is the genesis of all that is noble in human existence.

Too short is life for anything void of love or inharmonious with love.

Everything that enters the loving heart transforms into what it is made of.

To live in a manner that signifies a life lived through the spiritual, one must give oneself wholly to the giving of oneself.

Love plus wisdom equals goodness.

The enlightened heart has no hype to sell to others, only to give what it has to give.

Dangers of life, like bombs falling all around one . . . still, the loving heart moves through the battlefield tending to the wounded, doing the work of love.

Though constantly breaking, how strong is the heart of empathy . . . the heart of love.

The gentlest of hearts are the strongest of hearts.

The heart that has found its way to love
is not an instrument of mere sentiment but
one of acquired wisdom, drawing its light
from the spiritual of life.

As there is brilliance of mind, so is there
brilliance of heart.

The mind can enjoy cleverness, but the heart
needs something more . . . it needs the wisdom
that dwells deeper, that holds the key to the
deepest loves and truths and joys.

When the ego of a life subsides, everything spiritual is ready to come to life.

There is a difference between being sensitive, and living Sensitivity; of being compassionate, and living Compassion.

The spiritual dimension of humankind is to be honored, cherished, served, but most of all to be expressed.

Blessed is the life whose greatest yearning
is to give.

Even with love in one's heart doors may
still close to one, but Life's door will always
be open, welcoming the life that is lived
through love.

One either settles into the animality of
human character or goes the way of the
spiritual.

All must eventually answer the question of
whether their primary interest in life is to
just have a good time, or to bring good
to the time in which they live.

Every life is born in a primitive state of being,
spiritually speaking. A life of depth, beauty
and meaning is attained when a level of spiritual
maturity is reached where the giving of oneself
takes precedent over the taking for oneself.

No greater blessings are there than the chance
to love, to give, to redeem, to grow.

It is from the capacity to grow that capacities for the profound are created.

Some people are ever creating new space in their lives to let in more light — to allow for greater love and understanding. Others are forever blocking openings where anything could get through that would contradict their preconceptions of the world.

When light meets darkness, darkness is overcome.

Like a candle that is never lit . . . the life that is lived without love.

Ego walks with its head held high yet always with its back to the sun.

Many steps are taken in life, but the ones that leave a lasting print are only those taken toward divine love, divine light.

The heart knows the way, has always
known the way, yet how often has it
not been followed.

Ego promises everything, but delivers
nothing of true and lasting value.

One leaves his life in the most dire of
spiritual poverty who has lived for the
pursuit of worldly power and gain.

The larger the ambition of the material world the more trivial to the spiritual eye.

Every life of transcendence is a life of giving.

More and more materially speaking, brings one less and less, spiritually speaking.

When one is focused on material wealth for oneself beyond the necessities of one's life, one is far from the direction of the knowing heart. When one is focused on earthly power and ambitions, craving the false treasures and ornaments of the world, one is far from the direction of the knowing, loving heart. (And when one is in this state one is yet unborn to Life's majesty.)

To realize that we are here for just a short while passing briefly through this life, and often reminding ourselves of this reality goes a long way in keeping at bay the banalities that plague the everyday world.

The enlightened heart can be in the presence of any physical surrounding and still be accompanied by grace.

For the enlightened heart it is not about fame or fortune, but contribution.

What is done for applause is not worthy of applause.

They who contribute as much of their energies as they can to the betterment of life would do what they do even without compensation for their service, doing the work that most needs to be done.

What is given from a spiritual place does not keep score of the giving; only the baseness from the goings-on in the arena of worldly ambition keeps score.

All that is given without love or what emanates from love is of little weight or matter beyond the day.

Of human life time levels all but its most noble aspirations.

The compass of the noble heart is forever pointing to love.

A friend ego is not to those whose journey is of the spiritual.

Where humility is absent what of grace can be found?

To have the power to take, yet give; to destroy, yet create; to deliver cruelty, yet extend kindness . . . this, the mark of the noble heart.

Where does one go who does not travel the path to Selflessness, on to the gardens of its love . . .

The life that is lived with growing enlightenment leaves in its wake a trail of goodness.

What is human life for but to strive for and cultivate its highest qualities, giving to Life its best?

Each generation is presented with new opportunities to improve the world, every person holding a responsibility to do what he or she is able to do to create a better world.

Great advancements have been made by humankind in technology and various studies and disciplines, but what can this mean without the development of its spiritual dimension, moved by the yearnings of the heart?

There is much in the human world that deserves to be deplored, to have the fury of wrath levelled upon it, but the way to lessening the evils is to give it more love, more kindness and compassion than it often merits, trying to show or teach a better way of living, of being, to help make, if only for a time, a wiser, more salutary environment in some part of this world, staying always aware, though never losing heart, that there will be more evils to encounter as one goes through the journey of one's life.

To live by the rule of action-reaction is to live in accord with the universe, but the physical universe is violent and indiscriminate, moving without aim or resolution, and if humankind is to survive, is to attain the needed measure of wisdom and enlightenment to achieve a lasting peace, it must live outside this rule, must transcend the mindless tit-for-tat that fuels the violence and destruction that threatens its very existence; must go the way of the heart.

Accept love's light, and be for life a light.

The final part of a last breath — an exhale —
a letting out — a giving back . . . like the
final summation of the best of human life —
a giving back to life.

Whoever you are, wherever you are, there is
work to be done in the service of love.

Love, in spite of.

Trust in the wisdom of the heart.

There comes a time when books must close,
words must cease, and for love to be the truth,
the light that guides the way.

ABOUT THE AUTHOR

Carroll Blair is an author of more than twenty books and the recipient of numerous awards. His work has been well endorsed and commendably reviewed. Among his titles cited for distinction are *Through the Shadows*, winner of the Pacific Book Awards, and *Quarter Notes*, winner of the Sharp Writ Book Awards. He is an alumnus of the Boston Conservatory and lives in Massachusetts.